HAPPY AS A SAND-BOY

EARLY
RAILWAY POSTERS

Front Cover

Company	Great Northern Railway
Title	Happy as a Sand-Boy
Displayed	1907
Size	63cm × 101cm
NRM Ref	86/38/263

National Railway Museum

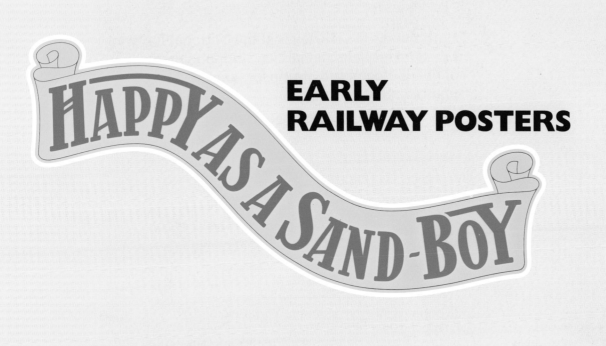

EARLY RAILWAY POSTERS

HAPPY AS A SAND-BOY

Beverley Cole and Richard Durack

London: HMSO

Acknowledgements

With thanks to colleagues at the National Railway Museum for help and advice, and to Lynn Patrick of the Photographic Studio for taking the photographs

© National Railway Museum, York 1990
First published 1990
British Library Cataloguing in Publication Data
A CIP catalogue record for this book is available from the British Library

Design: HMSO Graphic Design, Dee Slater

HMSO publications are available from:

HMSO Publications Centre
(Mail and telephone orders only)
PO Box 276, London, SW8 5DT
Telephone orders 071–873 9090
General enquiries 071–873 0011
(queuing system in operation for both numbers)

HMSO Bookshops
49 High Holborn, London, WC1V 6HB 071–873 0011 (counter service only)
258 Broad Street, Birmingham, B1 2HE 021–643 3740
Southey House, 33 Wine Street, Bristol, BS1 2BQ (0272) 264306
9–21 Princess Street, Manchester, M60 8AS 061–834 7201
80 Chichester Street, Belfast, BT1 4JY (0232) 238451
71 Lothian Road, Edinburgh, EH3 9AZ 031–228 4181

HMSO's Accredited Agents
(see Yellow Pages)

and through good booksellers

ISBN 0 11 290488 2
Printed in England for HMSO
Dd 291751 C90 5/90

Contents

Introduction

Early Years

'Few forms of advertisement by affiche lend themselves so completely to delicacy and refinement as the railway poster, which, for obvious reasons deals with all that is beautiful and attractive in nature, and commands attention in proportion to its originality of design and charm of colour. It has been said that there is no truer test of the character of a nation than its cuisine. It may today be averred with equal force that the pictorial poster enables one to judge fairly of the artistic progress of any given people and the well-directed energy of any given railway company.'[1]

F C G Marks

F C G Marks, writing in the *Great Western Railway Magazine* in 1907, may have allowed himself to get carried away a little with his subject but he was not the only writer to be concerned about the artistic standard of the railway poster. The railway poster was still in its infancy in the early years of this century but it was to develop into a familiar feature of station booking halls and platforms as the railway companies enticed passengers with an almost endless variety of colourful and evocative images. Some of the finest poster artists of the day were employed to portray the delights and temptations that lay beyond the facade of the local station. Above all the railway poster came to be associated with a world of sunshine, sandy beaches and endless fun. And in the years before the First World War the train was quite simply almost the only way to get there.

Railways had not always been so keen to advertise their services. The opening of the first public railways, particularly the Liverpool and Manchester Railway in 1830, had created such a wave of interest that publicity was hardly needed. The early railways did however feel a need to communicate with their passengers and one of the ways in which they did this was through the printed notice. Cheap to print, easy to display and with a large captive audience, the notice was the ideal way not only to convey information but also to keep passengers in order. Details of train services and fares alternated with warnings of dire penalties should the unfortunate passenger smoke, spit, trespass, cross the line (other than where allowed), join the train while in motion or in any other way disobey company regulations. Fraud and theft were of particular concern. Imprisonment and even transportation could be the result of travelling without a ticket or stealing company property.

As more lines opened, and the railway became less of a novelty, companies felt the need to publicise their services more. Newspaper advertising and the production of leaflets and handbills became more common. Commercial publishers too saw possibilities and guides to services and facilities were produced. The notice began to be used mainly to advertise services and it developed into an elaborate affair with woodcut illustrations, varieties of text and often a tinted background. But developments in colour lithography in the later years of the century were to make the notice largely obsolete and revolutionise the world of advertising.

Developments in Colour Lithography

Lithography had been invented almost a hundred years earlier by Alois Senefelder who, according to his own account,[2] conceived the idea while writing down a laundry list for his mother. He developed a simple process based on the principle that greasy substances attract one another while grease and water repel one another. The lithographic stones were first cut into blocks and then ground until the surface was smooth. The design was drawn onto the surface in reverse using a greasy drawing medium. This medium varied from printer to printer but Marks described a mixture composed of 'tallow, soap, wax, shellac and lamp black'.[3] The surface of the stone was then dampened with water which settled only on the unmarked area as it was repelled by the medium. It was then rolled over with greasy printing ink, which stuck to the medium while the water repelled it from the other areas, and the design was printed onto paper.

Colour lithography followed the same principle but was more elaborate. The design was again drawn onto a stone which became known as the key-stone. Impressions were taken from the key-stone and the design transferred onto separate colour stones on which the areas of each colour were drawn in. The stones were inked and printed in sequence onto a single sheet of paper. Care had to be taken in the order that the colours were printed as the colour stones were used not only for new colours but also to vary the colours that had already been printed. Blue was often printed over yellow to produce green and it was in fact possible to create an almost endless variety of shades and tints. Colour lithography came to be used increasingly for high quality illustrations but it was generally too expensive for commercial work although some bills and notices were produced. This changed towards the end of the century as technical developments, including the introduction of zinc plates, the use of powered printing presses and improvements in the lithographic process, combined to make the colour poster a cheap and effective form of advertising.

Much of the pressure for improvements in the printing process had come from the advertising industry of late Victorian Britain. The growing population and rising standard of living of this era had led to the growth of advertising on an unprecedented scale. The poster – colourful, cheap and easy to display – was an ideal way to advertise and soon there was a demand for more and more sites. The railway companies were not slow to realise the opportunities for increased revenue that poster advertising offered. Stations, both inside and out, were soon covered by posters advertising an intoxicating range of goods including dessicated soups, smoking mixtures, washing flannel, grate enamel, whalebone corsets, carbolic tooth powder and assorted pills, potions and ointments. The story of the foreign visitor who complained that too many stations had the name Bovril is probably apochryphal but it was not unusual for station names and signs to be pasted over as advertisers sought to use every available inch of space.

The Railway Companies

Railways had helped to create much of the country's prosperity. The system had grown rapidly but in an unplanned and haphazard way. The building and operating of lines was in the hands of private companies and by the middle of the nineteenth century a basic network had been established. In the following years further lines were constructed although many of these only duplicated existing routes and were built by rival companies to gain more business. Lines were also built through sparsely-populated rural areas and were often uneconomic from the outset. By 1914 the network consisted of over 20,000 miles of track and few towns or villages, except those in remote areas, were more than a few miles from their nearest station.

In spite of mergers and amalgamations there were still well over a hundred companies providing services at this time. These companies varied greatly in both size and character. In England four companies – the Great Western Railway, London and North Western Railway, Midland Railway and North Eastern Railway – owned over half the total system. The largest of these was the London and North Western which not only boasted of being the leading railway company in Britain but also the largest joint stock corporation in the world. Formed in 1846 by the amalgamation of four existing companies, including the Liverpool and Manchester Railway, the London and North Western went on to take control of more than forty other independent companies. It provided services in London, the Midlands, North Wales and north-west England as well as extending into South Wales and Yorkshire. In 1910 it owned 1,737 miles of track which it operated with over 3,000 locomotives and 10,000 carriages. At the other end of the scale railway services on the Isle of Wight were provided by two companies. The Isle of Wight Central Railway, formed by the amalgamation of three companies in 1887, operated services on just over twenty one miles of track with ten locomotives, two steam motor cars and fifty two carriages. It also provided services over a further nineteen miles of track on behalf of two other companies. The Isle of Wight Railway operated less than fifteen miles of track on the eastern side of the island with eight locomotives and sixty two carriages.

Between these extremes were companies of varying size providing services appropriate to the area they served. Many were based in industrial areas and generated most of their income from freight traffic. The Lancashire and Yorkshire Railway derived much of its income from carrying coal and coke although it also served the resorts of the Lancashire coast. The North Staffordshire Railway too drew much of its revenue from coal traffic. In contrast both the London Brighton and South Coast Railway, which served Sussex and the south coast, and the Great Eastern Railway, serving East Anglia, operated services in rural areas and the suburbs of London and relied for most of their income on passengers. In Scotland the Caledonian Railway and North British Railway were dominant while in Ireland services were provided by over twenty companies.

Competition and Rivalry

The existence of so many companies brought both benefits and disadvantages. Towns that were served by two or more companies could gain from good services and competitive fares but they could also suffer poor services from both. Towns served by one company were as likely to be happy with the service they received as unhappy. Much depended on the company or companies concerned and they ranged from the enterprising to the inefficient in the services they provided. As the century progressed much competition only served to weaken the companies involved. In Kent the South Eastern Railway and the London Chatham and Dover Railway provided their own services between most of the major towns and London with the result that neither made enough money to operate an efficient system and both were the subject of constant criticism. The two companies finally entered into a working union in 1899 and formed the South Eastern and Chatham Railway.

Elsewhere ambitious schemes were proposed that made little or no progress. The Lancashire Derbyshire and East Coast Railway had been formed to build a route for coal traffic from Lancashire to the Lincolnshire coast and in 1897 it opened its first stretch of line from Chesterfield to Lincoln. It got no further. It was unable to raise further capital and was bought by the Great Central Railway, with which it had been intended to compete, in 1906. The companies themselves did often try to avoid wasteful competition and saw advantages in promoting joint lines, amalgamations and working agreements. The Great Northern Railway and Midland Railway joined forces to form the Midland and Great Northern Joint Railway which operated a route across Norfolk. The London and North Western Railway tried unsuccessfully to amalgamate with the Lancashire and Yorkshire Railway in 1871 although it did take over the management of the North London Railway in 1909. The Great Central Railway, Great Eastern Railway and Great Northern Railway proposed to amalgamate in the years before the First World War but were not allowed by Parliament to proceed.

For the passenger life could be confusing. The overlapping of areas served by the companies meant that it was often not clear where the system of one company ended and another began. The companies themselves were not beyond exaggerating the importance of their systems and the guides and maps that they produced often suggested that their lines extended far beyond their boundaries. H J Jewell, writing in the Jubilee of the *Railway News* in 1914, recalled an unfortunate incident involving a customer who had enquired about train services from London to the west of England. 'On being informed that the district in regard to which she was enquiring was not served by the company, she advanced an opinion on the company's map which cannot be reproduced here as it verges on the libellous.'[4]

Passengers travelling any distance usually had to travel over the lines of more than one company. Through booking meant that a ticket could be bought to the final destination but it was still necessary to change trains when moving from the system of one company to another. Many companies however provided through services and carriages to avoid the need to change. The Great Northern Railway was able to advertise a direct service from London to Harrogate even though its system did not extend that far (plates 42 and 46). Its trains ran on to Harrogate by agreement with the North Eastern Railway who served the town. Both the Great Central Railway and the Midland Railway were able to advertise Blackpool even though neither company had lines running there (plates 1 and 47). The Great Central provided a wide range of tourist and cross-country expresses and ran services to destinations as far afield as Ilfracombe, Aberystwyth, Newcastle upon Tyne, Scarborough, Cromer and Bournemouth.

Routes to Scotland

Some of the most intense competition of these years took place on the routes between England and Scotland. The East Coast route was operated by the Great Northern Railway, North Eastern Railway and North British Railway and ran via York, Newcastle upon Tyne and Berwick. Services on the West Coast route were provided by the London and North Western Railway and the Caledonian Railway and its trains ran via Rugby, Preston and Carlisle. A third route was operated by the Midland Railway through Sheffield and Leeds to Carlisle. Services were then taken on either to Glasgow by the Glasgow and South Western Railway through Kilmarnock or to Edinburgh by the North British Railway through Hawick.

Each route had its own loyal customers and each was promoted enthusiastically by the companies concerned through posters and guides. The East Coast route styled itself the 'Shortest and Quickest' (plates 3 and 14) while the Midland, which had a longer route through more difficult country, was promoted as the most 'Interesting and Attractive' (plate 14) although it also became the most 'Direct and Picturesque' (plate 12) for the Burns country of Ayrshire and the Scott country of the Borders. The North British Railway, with lines to both Berwick and Carlisle, was in the position of being able to advertise both routes in the posters that it produced.

Speed in itself was not seen as an ideal way to attract passengers at this time and the companies were far keener to emphasize the standard of comfort and the facilities that they offered on their trains. Both the East Coast route and the North British Railway drew attention on their posters to the 'dining cars, sleeping cars and lavatory carriages' (plate 12) that they ran on their services and these had all been comparatively recent innovations. The North British was the first company in Britain to introduce sleeping cars in 1873 and the West Coast companies followed shortly afterwards. These were also the first carriages running in regular service to be equipped with lavatories. The provision of lavatories had always been a delicate subject and no satisfactory solution was found until carriages with a corridor along the side and a lavatory at each end were introduced. The corridor train, with covered gangways between the carriages, also enabled dining car services to develop and were first introduced onto the East and West Coast routes in 1893.

Much of the credit for improving standards was due to the Midland Railway which, in an attempt to win passengers for its long distance services, had introduced better carriages and facilities for both its first and third class passengers. Rival companies had been forced to follow and by the early years of the present century travelling to Scotland had become a pleasure rather than the ordeal it had been only a few years before. George Eyre-Todd, writing in *Scotland for the Holidays* (the guide to the West Coast route), described the delights of such a journey in 1914:

'The northward journey of eight hours or so is a thing of real pleasure in itself. Travelling in a train de luxe, with all the amenities of a first class hotel on board – kitchens, dining rooms, smoking-rooms, and hot and cold water lavatories; roomy deep cushioned compartments to read or chat in during the day, and snug berths to slumber in during the night; with, as long as daylight lasts, an unmatched panorama of some of the fairest scenery in the world sweeping ever before his eyes – the holidaymaker may well count the delights of his recess begun from the moment he sets foot in the North express.'[5]

Shipping

The railway companies did not confine their activities to the rails. They also operated a range of services to support their main business and had interests in canals, docks, ferries and road haulage. Most owned hotels and others, including the Great Western Railway, ran their own bus services. Steamships were also operated, for both passengers and freight, including services across the English Channel, North Sea and to Ireland.

At first the companies had rarely been allowed to operate their own vessels but this rule was eventually relaxed by Parliament and in the 1860s they began to build up their fleets. By the turn of the century cross-Channel services were being provided by the South Eastern and Chatham Railway from Dover and Folkestone, London Brighton and South Coast Railway from Newhaven and London and South Western Railway from Southampton. The Great Eastern Railway was the main operator of services across the North Sea. It ran its first vessels from Harwich in 1863 and over the next twenty years built up its traffic to Antwerp and Rotterdam to such an extent that it had to construct new facilities for its ships at Parkeston Quay, two miles west of the town, in 1882 (plate 28). Services were further improved when the Dutch authorities created a new port at the Hook of Holland eleven years later. The Great Central Railway also provided services to Antwerp, Rotterdam and Hamburg from Manchester via Grimsby. Services to Ireland were operated from Fleetwood jointly by the London and North Western Railway and Lancashire and Yorkshire Railway and from Holyhead by the London and North Western Railway. In the years before the first World War further services were added by the Midland Railway from Heysham and by the Great Western Railway from Fishguard.

More modern ships were gradually introduced onto these services. The early years of the present century saw the appearance of turbine-driven vessels which provided both a faster and more reliable service. The South Eastern and Chatham Railway became the first company to operate a turbine-driven ship when it introduced 'The Queen' onto its cross-Channel service in 1903. It was an immediate success and 'The Queen', according to a later article in the *Railway and Travel Monthly*, 'weathered her first gale in August splendidly, for, while the Ostend packet was five hours on her passage, and the Calais steamer 'Le Nord' was over an hour late, 'The Queen' crossed the Channel in a minute under the hour, and arrived at Calais with a dry upper deck.'[6] The company later issued a poster for the French market advertising its 'Grand Bateaux a Turbines' and featuring elegant passengers promenading aboard 'The Queen' to a background of heavy seas (plate 13). Most other companies introduced turbine steamers into their fleets in the following years and many of these vessels set new standards of comfort and luxury. The 'St Petersburg', built in 1910 and operated by the Great Eastern Railway, possessed 'many of the latest features of an Atlantic liner' including 'two promenade decks, an awning deck forming a spacious and covered promenade, a luxuriously fitted lounge, a smoking room with domed roof and wainscotted walls and a large and artistically decorated dining room'.[7]

The companies also built up their connections with the liner trade and both issued their own posters and overprinted information onto posters already published by the shipping companies. The South Eastern and Chatham Railway promoted several services including those of the American Line from Southampton, which had originally been founded as the Inman Line in 1886 to operate an emigrant and passenger trade between Liverpool and New York (plate 35). Southampton Docks, acquired by the London and South Western Railway in 1892, were actively developed in the years before the First World War and took much business from Liverpool despite the efforts of the London and North Western Railway on behalf of the northern port.

Growth of Resorts

It was above all with holiday travel that the railway poster came to be associated. Growing prosperity led to an increased demand for travel although the companies had not always been keen to cater for holiday traffic. Many had seen excursion trains as frivolous and an interference in the proper running of their railway, but gradually they came to be seen as an important source of revenue. The companies were in the fortunate position before the First World War of having few competitors for this traffic. It was still a time when the North British Railway was able to advertise the Motor Exhibition at Olympia happy in the knowledge that the motor car was still a novelty for the rich rather than a serious rival (plate 14).

The rapid growth of seaside resorts owed much to the expansion of the railway network. Sea bathing had increased in popularity after 1800 and railways were able to provide fast access from the towns and cities. The new visitors that the railways brought were not always welcomed with open arms. At Bridlington day visitors were disliked by regular visitors and residents alike and the station was sited well away from the sea. Most of the larger resorts, including Hastings and Scarborough, came to cater for all classes of visitor but others tried to retain a more select clientele.

Blackpool at first tried the same approach but eventually gave up the struggle and turned itself into the popular resort par excellence. The railway had first reached the town in 1846 and by 1880 Blackpool had over one million visitors a year. By the early years of the present century this figure had tripled and the two main stations in the town, with a total of twenty-nine platforms, were dealing with up to eighty excursions a day at busy times, in addition to regular services. The *Railway and Travel Monthly* described the promenade at this time as 'the finest in the world' and the town had amusements to match:

'At the Winter Gardens and the Tower a continuous round of gaiety is kept up. The best of everything can be heard and seen, from Tetrazzini and the most popular comedian to the latest sensation. At each of these places, too, a magnificent ballroom is attached for those who are disciples of "Terpichore", and at the Grand Theatre and Opera House, the latest London successes are engaged.'[8]

For those not wishing to 'mix with the madding crowd' the more sedate resorts of St Annes and Lytham were easily at hand.

Elsewhere on the Lancashire coast both Morecambe and Southport also grew as resorts although not on the same scale. Morecambe was served by the Midland Railway from Skipton and the West Riding, as well as by the London and North Western Railway, and drew so many of its visitors from Yorkshire that it came to be known as Bradford-by-the-Sea. Southport catered for both fashionable visitors and trippers and was unique in providing an Excursionists' Day Nursery where children under five could be left while their parents enjoyed themselves. It was also promoted as an all-the-year-round resort particularly suitable for those who disliked the rigours of the English winter (plate 45). Visitors were assured that winters were 'comparatively mild' and that if 'a shower should happen to fall, the porous nature of the soil ensures that it shall not have a permanent effect upon the health and spirits. Many of the main streets have an almost continuous verandah, under which exercise may be had at all times.'[9]

Inland resorts expanded too. Harrogate, which boasted over eighty mineral springs, doubled its number of visitors after the first line was opened to the town in 1849. Further increases encouraged the building of the 'most handsomely appointed bathing establishments in Great Britain' where facilities included 'natural sulphur water baths, vapour baths, needle baths, hot and cold douches, inhalation and pulverisation rooms and every modern method with latest improved appliances'.[10] Remote areas were made more accessible by the railway although the companies had often faced difficulties in building their lines. The Peak District, Lake District, North Wales and the mountains, lochs and glens of Scotland were all promoted as ideal places to indulge in such healthy pursuits as walking, boating and fishing. Golf was becoming increasingly popular and the Scottish companies in particular were to the fore in advertising the courses they served and the facilities offered. But such activities were not compulsory. For the less active visitor motor tours and steamer trips were always available.

In some cases railways created resorts where little had existed before. Skegness in 1871 had a population of less than five hundred. A line was opened to the town two years later and a large station built with the hope of attracting holiday traffic to the sandy beaches. The crowds came and facilities grew. By 1907 Skegness was attracting 300,000 visitors a year, mostly from the east Midlands and Yorkshire although many also travelled from London on the popular three-hour excursions that the Great Northern Railway had introduced in 1905 (frontispiece). The North Staffordshire Railway in contrast had no access to the sea and chose instead to develop Rudyard Lake as an inland resort (plate 41). The Lake itself had been created in 1793 to supply the Trent and Mersey Canal. Boating and fishing were available to visitors as well as a golf club with an annual subscription of one guinea for gentlemen and half a guinea for ladies. The company also built the Hotel Rudyard which, according to the Official Guide to the North Staffordshire Railway, catered for 'parties of all kinds. The humble labourer with his wife and family out for the day, get their tea-water or bread and cheese lunch; and the wealthy manufacturer or merchant his table d'hôte'.[11]

The First Posters

The first railway posters to appear came in for much criticism. Norman Wilkinson (1878–1971), later to produce some of the finest railway posters, wrote of an 'uninspired jumble of small views of resorts, frequently arranged in little circular frames, with a good deal of meaningless decoration interwoven between each picture. The effect was a hotch-potch which was quite unintelligable at a distance'.[12] Others were even more scathing. 'In geometrical spaces, mostly circles and ellipses, are shown interminable piers straggling through the bluest of seas; a patch of yellow indicates miles of sand for the spade of the infant; sky-high hotels, birds eye views of severely laid out flower beds, bandstands, and the like, are the items on which the changes have been rung for years'.[13] Most of the early posters that were produced lacked inspiration. Companies issued posters which, like the notices they replaced, tried to crowd as much information as possible into the available space. It was many years before image and text were to be used effectively.

Nevertheless many of these posters appear charming today even though they may have failed to capture the attention of the passenger of the time. The poster produced by the Midland Railway featuring 'Tourist Resorts in the Peak of Derbyshire' contains a series of colourful views of local attractions including a Midland express crossing Monsal Dale Viaduct (plate 7). 'England's Garden Isle', issued by the Isle of Wight companies as late as 1914, provides a fascinating glimpse of the Edwardian seaside with its bathing machines and paddle steamers (plate 39). Most of the images used in these years were provided by printers and the railway companies were often dependant for the standard of their posters on the printers that they employed. Printers were usually asked to submit designs for approval and these were often either stock views or cheap commissions from artists. It was not a system that encouraged innovation although some printers did produce adventurous work and, in a number of cases, were responsible for persuading companies to adopt poster advertising.

The companies themselves rarely commissioned artists at this time. Artists were encouraged to submit speculative designs in the hope that they might be used and Norman Wilkinson recalled how he had sent a design of a steamship on the Heysham to Belfast crossing to the Advertising Manager of the Midland Railway. It was received without enthusiasm and Wilkinson was offered seven guineas for it which he refused. Instead he sent it to the Great Eastern Railway. 'A very slight alteration to the funnel markings and a minor addition to the superstructure made it into a GER vessel.'[14] The Great Eastern were impressed and published it as a poster. Also impressed were the Directors of the Midland Railway who instructed their Advertising Manager to write to Wilkinson asking why their company could not have posters of such a high standard.

A More Professional Approach

Slowly a more professional approach to advertising began to emerge during the early years of the present century. Many companies created their own advertising departments and appointed advertising managers to put their publicity on a surer footing. There was a move away from the use of agents, and companies began to control the whole of their advertising output. Effort was directed towards persuading passengers to travel rather than just providing information on services. A new attitude to travel as a pleasurable experience in itself began to develop and was encouraged by the appearance of journals such as the *Railway Magazine* and *Railway and Travel Monthly*. Companies became anxious to establish their own identity and make both themselves and the services that they offered more familiar. The Great Western Railway began to style itself the 'Holiday Line' and used this slogan on much of its advertising. The Lancashire and Yorkshire became the 'Business Line' and the London Brighton and South Coast the 'Sunshine Line'. The Caledonian Railway was promoted as the 'True Line' and its passengers travelled with 'True Convenience, True Comfort, True Economy and True to Time'.

There were other innovations too. Travel offices run by the railway companies were opened in large towns and cities. Cooperation with local advertising associations was built up. Lantern slides of resorts were lent to interested groups and there was increased participation at exhibitions and displays. The Lancashire and Yorkshire Railway opened advertising kiosks on the promenade at Southport and in Manchester while at Victoria Station in London the London Brighton and South Coast Railway installed 'a novel advertising device' consisting of a

'large bas-relief enclosed in a wooden frame and so arranged as to be illuminated alternately from opposite sides. When lit up from the left side, a prepossessing young lady is shown, enquiring "For Brighton?" whilst the illumination of the other side reveals one of the railway company's porters, who, in giving the required information, adds the comment "and health and sunshine, Miss".'[15]

The Great Western Railway in 1907 sent one of its Milner Daimler omnibuses on a tour of Scotland to distribute advertising literature. It left Slough in early November and encountered four foot snowdrifts on the road to Inverness before returning forty six days later. Several companies also made attempts to improve the appearance of advertisements on stations and the North Eastern Railway introduced a scheme using standard colours for display boards and regulating the sites where posters could be exhibited.

The amount of advertising material produced by the companies increased enormously in both quality and quantity. New forms of publicity began to appear including postcards and carriage panels containing advertisements and photographs of resorts. The range of guides and pamphlets became almost endless and began to extend beyond resorts and holiday areas. Anglers, cyclists and golfers were all catered for and the Great Estern Railway published a handbook for passengers on its continental services giving details of how Tokyo could be reached in only seventeen days via Harwich and the Trans-Siberian Railway. There was also a move towards more coordinated campaigns involving the use of a range of publicity material. The North Estern Railway in 1913 issued its booklet *Alice in Holidayland* describing Alice's adventures on holiday on the Yorkshire coast and parodying the work of Lewis Carroll and the drawings of Sir John Tenniel. The booklet contained illustrations by Frank Mason (1876–1965) and several of these were printed as posters including those featuring the Walrus and the Carpenter at Scarborough and Tweedledum and Tweedledee on the beach at Bridlington (plates 31 and 32). A large poster for street hoardings, printed in twenty-four sheets, was also produced and the Great Northern Railway overprinted copies of the posters for use on its own system.

Image and Content

The poster played an increasingly important role in advertising campaigns and there was a great deal of discussion about what constituted a good poster and who it should be aimed at. 'The Advertising Manager has to bear in mind that his traffic is drawn from the masses, the middle classes and the aristocracy'[16] wrote H J Jewell of the Great Northern Railway in 1914 and the companies tried, by the breadth and range of their advertising, to appeal to all their potential customers in turn. There was general agreement that the first object of a poster was to catch the eye and that the attention should be drawn from the image to the lettering. 'The most successful form of poster from the public concept is one which pictorially depicts a terse and telling phrase'[17] wrote Jewell again. If it could have artistic merit as well so much the better.

Most of the images used on railway posters were both tasteful and restrained. Landscapes were common as were views of resorts. Figures appeared rarely unless they were part of the general scene. There was little use of the seductive female figure that was so common in the posters produced by the French railway companies at this time. The aim above all else was to appeal to families and by emphasising the open space and fresh air of country and seaside the companies were able to provide a vivid contrast with the conditions in most towns and cities. Images of children playing on the beach became a familiar feature in the advertising of resorts and there was much stress on the benefits of the healthy outdoor life. There was less of the exaggeration that was common in other advertising posters of the period although occasionally there were what would be seen today as lapses of taste. The Lancashire and Yorkshire Railway issued a poster in 1914 drawing attention to the safety of railways compared to the new forms of transport by road and air. It featured views of a pilot falling from an aeroplane, an overturned car with its occupants in a river and a Lancashire and Yorkshire express speeding towards its destination, with the caption:

'Some people travel by aeroplane,
And others travel by car,
But those who desire comfort with speed,
Travel by L&YR.'[18]

Some of the posters that combined image and text most successfully were produced by the Great Northern Railway. 'Skegness is So Bracing' by John Hassall, which first appeared in 1908 and featured the figure of the jolly fisherman skipping along the beach, was the most famous of these but there were many others and several of the subjects that were introduced were developed over the years. 'Happy as a Sand-Boy' was issued in 1907 and showed a small boy playing on the beach at Skegness with a bucket and spade. Two years later in 'Still a Happy Sand-Boy' he was back but this time he had built a Great Northern Railway 4-4-2 locomotive and carriage. Both the Great Eastern Railway and the North Eastern Railway published effective posters, featuring golden sands and bracing air, for the east coast resorts that they served but other companies found it more difficult. A good image was often spoilt by an uninspired slogan and some that appeared stretched the imagination. The Great North of Scotland Railway promoted the Moray Firth Coast as the 'Scottish Riviera' while, in the hands of the Furness Railway, Grange-over-Sands became the 'Naples of the North'. Things were little better in the south where Ashdown Forest in Sussex was advertised by the London Brighton and South Coast Railway as the 'Sussex Highlands'.

The companies were often keen to associate the areas they served with the great literary and historical figures of the past. The North British Railway advertised the 'Home and Haunts of Sir Walter Scott' (plate 12) while the Glasgow and South Western Railway countered with the 'Land o'Burns' (plate 37). The Donegal Railway promoted north-west Ireland as the 'Land of Tyrconnel' (plate 6). In England the coast of Kent became 'Caesar's Choice!' (plate 33) while passengers on the Midland and Great Northern Joint Railway passed through 'Poppyland' and 'Broadland' on their way to 'Dickensland' (plate 38). Royal and aristocratic connections were also stressed. The Midland and Great Northern line, which passed close to the royal residence of Sandringham, became the 'Royal Route to Broadland' (plate 15) while the Lancashire Derbyshire and East Coast Railway styled itself the 'Dukeries Route' (plate 2).

The emphasis was very much on persuading passengers to holiday at home, although many companies also advertised continental attractions. Ullswater was promoted by the Great Northern Railway as 'The English Lucerne,' a cheaper if less fashionable alternative to Switzerland (plate 4). Harrogate became 'Britain's 100% Spa' (plate 46) and 'Britain's Health Resort' (plate 42). 'No Briton need cross the waters to take the cure', wrote the *Railway and Travel Monthly* confidently, 'whether he be in search of fashionable society, better waters or more attractive surroundings. Harrogate, the 'Queen of English Watering Places', can give him a variety of cures, to obtain which abroad one would need to scour half the continent.'[19] The Great Western Railway promoted the 'Cornish Riviera' with the slogan 'See your own Country First.' Posters and booklets featuring elegant visitors strolling beneath palm trees were used to provide a favourable comparison with the Mediterranean. An advertisement printed on enamel sheet stressed the similarities 'in shape, climate and natural beauties' between Cornwall and Italy while a poster showing almost identical views of the Home and Continental Rivieras asked the question 'Where's the Difference?' The *Railway and Travel Monthly* was less impressed. 'Those who go to Falmouth, St Ives or Penzance hoping to find the brilliant sunshine of Cannes or Nice in February will be mostly disappointed.' And it added ominously, 'Rain is not uncommon.'[20]

Posters and other publicity material were also sent abroad to tempt visitors to Britain, although the companies were often accused of not making enough effort in this direction. Joint advertising with shipping companies and overseas railway companies was sometimes used and the South Eastern and Chatham Railway joined forces with the Northern Railway of France to promote the resorts of Kent and Sussex. As part of the campaign the South Eastern and Chatham reprinted its poster 'Herne Bay's Industry is Health-Making' with lettering in French above and below the image although how many visitors flocked to Herne Bay as a result is not known (plate 10). And efforts were not only confined to Europe. Several companies, ranging from the Great Western Railway to the Stratford-upon-Avon and Midland Junction Railway, published guides for American visitors and emphasised their association with such celebrities as William Shakespeare and George Washington.

'The Advertising Man'

The move towards greater professionalism in advertising saw the emergence of a new type of railway official and it was not long before calls were being made for professional recognition. The *Railway Gazette* ran a series of letters in 1911 asking the question 'Is the Railway Advertising Man properly recognised as a force in modern railway work?' Most correspondents thought not and argued that it was time that their special skills and expert knowledge were properly appreciated. Railway advertising certainly enjoyed a much higher profile during these years and the appointment of an advertising manager would often transform both the approach to advertising within a company and its effectiveness. This growing importance led to greater confidence and encouraged many of the companies to become more adventurous in their work. Not only did more imaginative posters begin to appear but there was also a willingness to tackle a wider range of subjects.

One of the first companies to move in this direction was the London and North Western Railway. As early as 1904 it produced a striking poster for its London to Manchester service featuring a front view of one of its new Precursor class 4-4-0 locomotives. In the following year it issued two posters by Norman Wilkinson advertising its steamship route between Holyhead and Dublin. In his autobiography Wilkinson recalled that he decided to approach the subject of the first poster 'To Ireland' with 'simplicity and truth' (plate 9). It was usual at this time for companies to insist that their vessels should look as large and impressive as possible but Wilkinson took a different view:

'How much better to make the steamer quite small, an

incident in the picture, and to concentrate on a really fine day in the Irish Channel, blue sea and a gentle breeze. I also decided to keep the lettering to an absolute minimum, small and simple in treatment.'[21]

The Directors were less impressed but accepted the advice of their General Manager that it should be published. Its appearance created an enormous amount of interest and was hailed by newspapers and others as the finest example yet of 'Art on the Hoardings'.

Encouraged by this reception the London and North Western went on to greatly expand its advertising. It issued a series of postcards of its locomotives, rolling stock and the resorts it served which proved extremely popular. It improved the standard of advertising on its road vehicles. The *North-Western News*, a newspaper for holidaymakers, was published and major campaigns were launched including one to promote the resorts of North Wales. When the Great Western Railway opened its shorter route to Birmingham it responded by drawing attention to the forty trains a day it ran on its own line and to the facilities they offered, including the services of a shorthand typist on many trains. In 1910 a further poster by Wilkinson was issued. 'The Best Permanent Way in the World' featured a section of the London and North Western main line between Stafford and Crewe and highlighted the reputation that the Company had for the good riding quality of its trains (plate 21). The *Railway Gazette* was full of praise for the subject matter and wrote approvingly:

We owe one especial debt of gratitude to the London and North Western Railway, which was one of the first railways in England to abolish from its hoardings pictorial representations of anaemic young ladies, who tend rather to frighten away passengers than bring traffic.'[22]

Other companies too began 'using the railway to advertise the railway'.[23] The Midland Railway issued a poster by Fred Taylor (1875–1963) of its London terminus at St Pancras featuring a panoramic view of the interior of the station 'on the eve of the departure of a Scotch express'[24] (plate 22). The view is both accurate and delightful in its detail although there is less smoke than might have been expected. The express for Scotland waits to leave from platform two on the departure side of the station while on the opposite side several trains have arrived from the north. Taylor has faithfully recorded many of the features unique to St Pancras including the cab road with its steps for passengers running between the platforms and, in the right foreground, one of the pony-drawn barrows that were used to convey parcels between trains and the Parcel Office.

Elsewhere the North London Railway chose to use one of its 4-4-0 tank locomotives to advertise its 'Open Air Route' to the City (plate 23) and the North Eastern Railway published a series of posters featuring 'airship views'[25] of ports on the North East coast (plate 20). The North Eastern relied for most of its income on freight traffic and produced a variety of publicity material aimed at commercial and industrial customers.

Forward Great Central

Some of the finest advertising of these years was produced by the Great Central Railway. Formed in 1900 the Great Central was not a new railway but had changed its name from the Manchester Sheffield and Lincolnshire Railway in the previous year after the completion of its extension to Marylebone Station in London. Its change of name reflected its change of status and the Great Central had been conceived on an ambitious scale to link with the South Eastern and Chatham Railway and a proposed channel tunnel to provide a through route between Manchester and Paris. It was a company anxious to establish itself and it produced a stream of inventive publicity to advertise its services.

A Publicity Department was created in 1902 and a large budget allocated to it. The Company soon booked advertising space on the windows of telephone kiosks throughout London and printed its posters on specially thin paper so that they would be better illuminated at night. Guides and booklets were produced for both passengers and commercial customers and a regular publication was issued for homebuyers who wanted to settle in the growing towns and suburbs along the line. Some of the most talented artists of the day were employed to produce posters that were both innovative and topical. In 1904 the Great Central issued a poster advertising the Cup Final which it pasted up outside its Manchester offices two weeks before the match. With the title 'Billy Meredith Secures the Cup' it showed the Manchester City player scoring the winning goal against Bolton Wanderers. In the match itself at the Crystal Palace he did just that and scored the only goal of the game although, as contemporary accounts record, there was a suspicion of offside. The Company also went in for publicity on a giant scale and in 1912 placed what was reputed to be the largest poster in the world outside its headquarters at Marylebone advertising the newly-opened Immingham Dock.

The Great Central put some of its best efforts into publicising its dock facilities at Grimsby and Immingham. It had had a long association with Grimsby and had developed it as a major port. Passenger services across the North Sea had been introduced in 1865 and a fleet of modern vessels was operated to Hamburg, Rotterdam and Antwerp. One of these, the SS Bury, featured in the poster and booklet that the Great Central published in 1911 under the title 'Step on at Grimsby for the Continent' (plate 26). The poster was an unusual design and showed an enormous pair of feet boarding the vessel in England while girls in national costume, a popular feature in advertising of the period, waved from the shores of Belgium, Holland and Germany. It drew a rare example of humour from the *Railway Gazette* which commented:

'It is to be hoped the Gulliver-like gentleman, whose nether extremities only are visible, will not swamp one of the Company's steamers.'[26]

Immingham, six miles west of Grimsby, was developed as a deep-water dock mainly to handle coal traffic and was opened in 1912. The Great Central produced a souvenir booklet to commemmorate the event and several of the illustrations by Fortunino Matania (1881–1963) were issued as posters including the view of the coaling jetty (plate 30).

The First World War and After

At the outbreak of war in September 1914 the government took control of the network although it left the running of the system to a Railway Executive Committee composed of general managers of several of the leading companies. Recruiting posters began to appear on stations but the *Railway and Travel Monthly* was still able to publish a full range of posters in its edition of July 1915. There was an emphasis on inland holidays rather than seaside resorts and Wales was recommended 'for tourists deprived of their annual visit to Switzerland'.[27] Soon a more sombre note was sounded. The first 'roll of honour' posters were issued with companies listing employees who had been killed or wounded serving with the armed forces. The

Great Northern Railway produced a poster giving details of decorations and medals awarded to company staff at the front. At the beginning of 1917 restrictions were placed on travel and fares were increased in an attempt to discourage passengers, although these had little effect.

The War left the railways badly run down. Income from government had not kept pace with costs and in addition the benefits of running the system as a coordinated network had become apparent. There was talk of state control continuing but this was rejected and instead four much larger, but still privately-owned, companies were formed by amalgamating the existing companies. This 'grouping' came into effect on 1 January 1923 and created the Great Western Railway (in an enlarged version), London and North Eastern Railway, London Midland and Scottish Railway and Southern Railway.

Holiday travel continued to be discouraged while the railways recovered after the War but by the early 1920s it was getting back into its stride. The *Railway Magazine*, in its review of Railway Art and Literature in 1922, was able to record 'some return to pre-war standards'[28] and describe the efforts of no fewer than sixteen companies. Little outstanding work was produced in the short period before the 'grouping' but some of the posters that were issued are not without interest. The Midland Railway issued the 'Peak District for Picture Makers' illustrating how photography had become a popular hobby (plate 48). The central figure, dressed as the 'Kodak' girl and destined to become a major feature of Kodak advertising, is about to take a photograph with her folding pocket camera. Photography had been given an enormous boost by the War as family snapshots were sent to the front and women were still buying more cameras than men at this time.

The railway poster was to take a very different course in the years after 1923. The new companies got off to a shaky start but they soon established their own distinct styles and were to raise the status of the railway poster to a higher level. Norman Wilkinson worked for the London Midland and Scottish Railway, where he became their most prolific artist, and both Frank Mason and Fred Taylor worked regularly for the London and North Eastern Railway. They were joined by some of the finest commercial artists of the day and the London and North Eastern Railway in particular was to set new standards in poster art with its often daring and innovative designs.

The National Railway Museum Collection

The posters in this book are all from the collection at the National Railway Museum in York. Many were kept by the companies themselves and have found their way to the Museum via British Rail and the former Museum of British Transport. Others have been donated by members of the public and the Museum has also purchased posters in recent years to fill significant gaps in the collection. Almost all were intended for display and their survival has been largely a matter of chance. Many were exhibited in travel offices and did not have to face the rigours of a station platform while others were sent abroad and have found their way back to this country in recent years. Two of the posters in this book – 'Morecambe Loosens you Stumps' and 'Loch Katrine via West Coast Route' – were found pasted under the poster 'Summer Breezes on the Wicklow Coast' while conservation work was being carried out. 'Loch Katrine' had suffered slight damage but the poster of Morecambe had been preserved in perfect condition and had retained much of its original colouring through being protected from the light for so long. All three were mounted onto new backings and, together with the rest of the collection, can look forward to a more secure future so that they can be enjoyed by future generations.

References

1 F C G Marks, 'The Evolution of the Pictorial Poster' in the *Great Western Railway Magazine*, May 1907, p99

2 Alois Senefelder, *Vollständiges Lehrbuch der Steindrucherei* (A Complete Course of Lithography), 1818

3 F C G Marks, 'The Evolution of the Pictorial Poster' in the *Great Western Railway Magazine*, May 1907, p100

4 H J Jewell, 'The Publicity Department' in the Jubilee of the *Railway News*, 1914, p215

5 George Eyre-Todd, *Scotland for the Holidays* published by the Caledonian Railway, 1914, pp4–5

6 G W Tripp, 'The Turbine Steamer' in the *Railway and Travel Monthly*, January 1912, pp49–50

7 'Twentieth Century Railway Development. No 7, The Great Eastern Railway' in the *Railway and Travel Monthly*, March 1911, pp191–192

8 H S Lawrence, 'To the Lancashire Seaside by the London and North Western Railway' in the *Railway and Travel Monthly*, August 1911, pp144–145

9 'To Southport by the Cheshire Lines' in the *Railway and Travel Monthly*, July 1913, p56

10 *North Eastern Railway Guide*, 1897, p18

11 *The Official Illustrated Holiday Guide to the North Staffordshire Railway*, second edition, 1891, p80

12 Norman Wilkinson, *A Brush with Life*, p19

13 W Gunn Gwennet, 'Artistic Railway Posters' in the *Railway Magazine*, November 1900, p416

14 Norman Wilkinson, *A Brush with Life*, p23

15 *Railway Gazette*, 20 December 1907, p597

16 H J Jewell, 'The Publicity Department' in the Jubilee of the *Railway News*, 1914, p217

17 H J Jewell, 'The Publicity Department' in the Jubilee of the *Railway News*, 1914, p217

18 *Railway Gazette*, 20 March 1914, p441

19 'Harrogate, England's Winter Spa' in the *Railway and Travel Monthly*, February 1911, p160

20 W J Scott, 'To the Cornwall Riviera in Winter by the "Riviera Limited"' in the *Railway and Travel Monthly*, January 1912, p2

21 Norman Wilkinson, *A Brush with Life*, pp19–20

22 *Railway Gazette*, 3 June 1910, p613

23 *Railway Gazette*, 3 June 1910, p613

24 James Scott, 'The Fascination of Railway Stations. No 5, St Pancras' in the *Railway and Travel Monthly*, February 1912, p93

25 *Railway Gazette*, 19 November 1909, pp694–695

26 *Railway Gazette*, 14 July 1911, p42

27 'The Railway Picture Gallery of 1915' in the *Railway and Travel Monthly*, July 1915, p9

28 'Railway Art and Literature in 1922' in the *Railway Magazine*, July 1922, p59

Further reading

Railway and Travel Monthly, 1910–1919, and *Transport and Travel Monthly*, 1920–1922

Railway Gazette, 1906–1922

Railway Magazine, 1897–1922

National Railway Museum, *The National Railway Collection*, Collins, 1988

J Simmons, *The Railway in England and Wales, 1830–1914*, Vol. 1, *The System and its Working*, Leicester University Press, 1978

J Simmons, *The Railway in Town and Country, 1830–1914*, David and Charles, 1986

John Barnicoat, *A Concise History of Posters*, Thames and Hudson, 1972

Walter Shaw Sparrow, *Advertising and British Art*, Bodley Head, 1924

J T Shackleton, *The Golden Age of the Railway Poster*, New English Library, 1976

Happy Holidays. The Golden Age of Railway Posters, introduction by Michael Palin, Pavilion Books, 1987

The Posters

Plate 1

Company Midland Railway

Title Blackpool. Health & Pleasure, Glorious Sea

Displayed Circa 1893

Printer Bemrose & Sons, Derby & London

Size 101cm × 63cm

NRM Ref 75/38/6

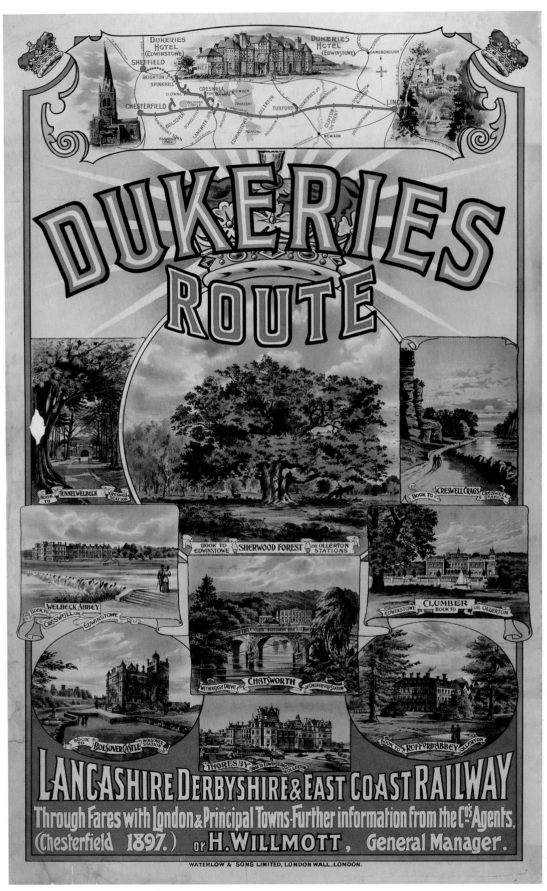

Plate 2

Company	Lancashire Derbyshire & East Coast Railway
Title	Dukeries Route
Displayed	1897
Printer	Waterlow and Sons Limited, London Wall, London
Size	65cm × 102cm
NRM Ref	88/38/46

Plate 3

Companies	Great Northern Railway, North Eastern Railway and North British Railway
Title	England and Scotland. East Coast Route
Displayed	Circa 1900
Printer	McCorquodale and Co Limited, Leeds
Size	64cm × 102cm
NRM Ref	83/38/209

Plate 4

Company	Great Northern Railway
Title	Ullswater 'The English Lucerne'
Displayed	1901
Printer	Andrew Reid & Co Ltd, 50 Grey Street, Newcastle-on-Tyne
Size	64cm × 94cm
NRM Ref	88/38/45

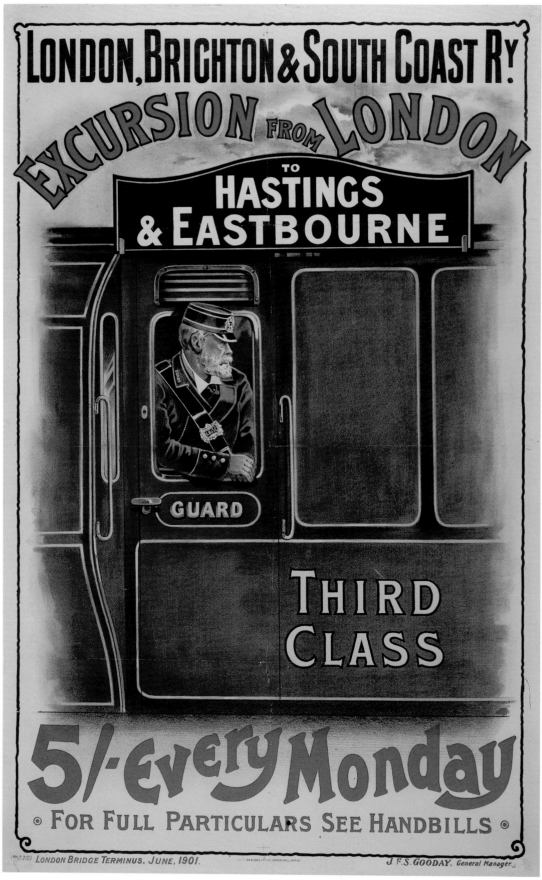

Plate 5

Company	London Brighton & South Coast Railway
Title	Excursions from London to Hastings and Eastbourne
Displayed	1901
Printer	Waterlow & Sons Limited, London Wall, London
Size	65cm × 101cm
NRM Ref	88/38/139

Plate 6

Company	Donegal Railway
Title	The North-West of Ireland
Displayed	Circa 1903
Printer	W Colhoun, Londonderry
Size	64cm × 102cm
NRM Ref	88/38/7

Plate 7

Company   Midland Railway
Title   Tourist Resorts in the Peak of Derbyshire
Displayed   Circa 1903
Printer   Bemrose & Sons Ltd, Derby, London & Watford
Size   67cm × 102cm
NRM Ref   87/38/4

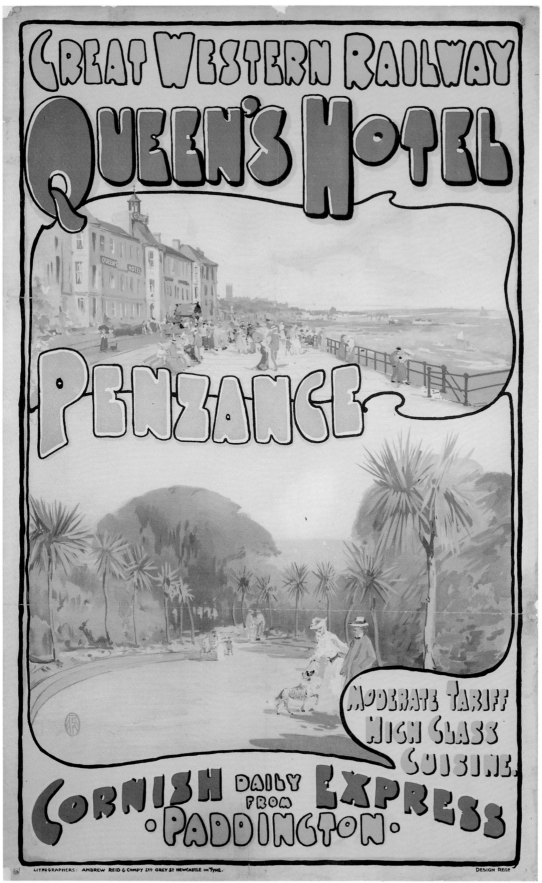

Plate 8

Company	Great Western Railway
Title	Queen's Hotel, Penzance
Artist	Alec Fraser
Displayed	Circa 1904
Printer	Andrew Reid & Company Ltd, Grey St, Newcastle-on-Tyne
Size	64cm × 102cm
NRM Ref	86/38/24

Plate 9

Company   London & North Western Railway   *Printer*   McCorquodale & Co Limited
Title   To Ireland   *Size*   160cm × 97cm
Artist   Norman Wilkinson   *NRM Ref*   79/38/452
Displayed 1905

Plate 10

Company   Chemins de Fer du Nord and South Eastern and Chatham Railway
Title   Herne Bay's Industry is 'Health Making'
Displayed Circa 1906
Size   64cm × 102cm
NRM Ref 86/38/62

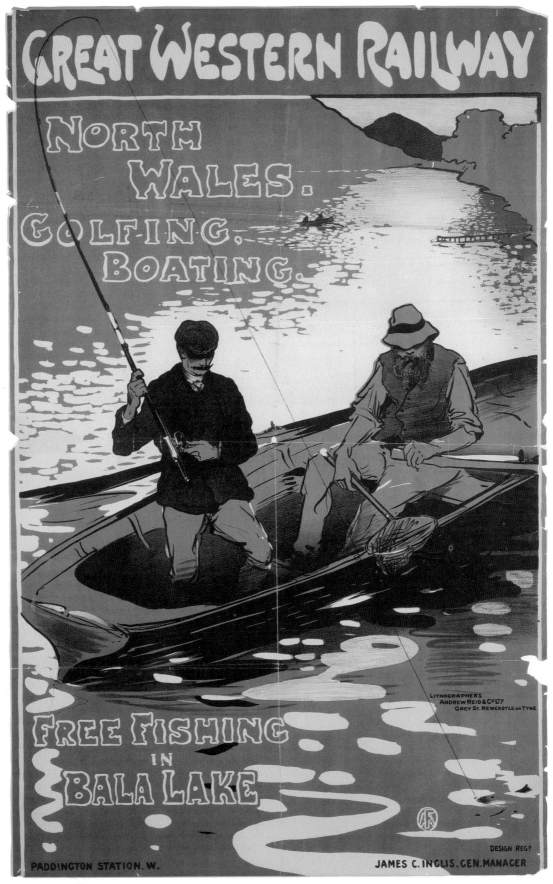

Plate 11

Company Great Western Railway
Title North Wales. Golfing, Boating, Free Fishing in Bala Lake
Artist Alec Fraser
Displayed 1907
Printer Andrew Reid & Co Ltd, Grey St, Newcastle-on-Tyne
Size 65cm × 101cm
NRM Ref 86/38/25

Plate 12

Company	North British Railway
Title	The Home and Haunts of Sir Walter Scott
Displayed	1907
Printer	W & A K Johnston Ltd, Edinburgh, Glasgow & London
Size	64cm × 101cm
NRM Ref	86/38/32

Plate 13

Company	South Eastern & Chatham Railway
Title	Grand Bateaux a Turbines. Calais-Douvres ou Boulogne–Folkestone
Displayed	1907
Printer	McCorquodale & Company Limited, St Thomas St, London, SE
Size	64cm × 102cm
NRM Ref	86/38/87

Plate 14

Company	North British Railway
Title	6th International Motor Exhibition, Olympia
Displayed	1907
Printer	Weiners P & A Co Ltd, London
Size	63cm × 102cm
NRM Ref	86/38/321

Plate 15

Company	Midland & Great Northern Joint Railways
Title	The Royal Route to Broadland
Displayed	Circa 1908
Printer	Sir Joseph Causton & Sons Limited, London
Size	64cm × 102cm
NRM Ref	88/38/47

Plate 16

Company	North Eastern Railway
Title	Scarborough Braces You Up. The Air Does It
Displayed	Circa 1909
Printer	Criterion Press, Leicester & London
Size	64cm × 102cm
NRM Ref	86/38/201

42

Plate 17

Company	London & North Western Railway
Title	Summer Breezes on the Wicklow Coast
Artist	F Whatley
Displayed	Circa 1909
Printer	McCorquodale & Co Limited, London
Size	61cm × 101cm
NRM Ref	78/38/1836

Plate 18

Company	London & North Western Railway
Title	Morecambe Loosens your Stumps!
Displayed	Circa 1909
Printer	Horrocks & Co Ltd, Ashton-U-Lyne
Size	63cm × 101cm
NRM Ref	88/38/72

44

Plate 19

Company   Caledonian Railway and London & North Western Railway
Title   Loch Katrine via West Coast Route
Displayed   Circa 1909
Printer   McCorquodale & Co Ltd, London
Size   63cm × 101cm
NRM Ref   88/38/73

Plate 20

Company	North Eastern Railway
Title	The Tees Ports, Hartlepool, and Middlesbrough, & the Railway Connections
Artist	Percy Home
Displayed	1909
Printer	Delittle, Fenwick & Co, York
Size	62cm × 100cm
NRM Ref	78/38/1078

THE BEST PERMANENT WAY IN THE WORLD.

Plate 21

Company London & North Western Railway
Title The Best Permanent Way in the World
Artist Norman Wilkinson
Displayed 1910

Printer McCorquodale & Co Limited
Size 160cm × 97cm
NRM Ref 79/38/340

GOING NORTH?

St PANCRAS

Plate 22

Company Midland Railway Size 125cm × 101cm
Title Going North? St Pancras NRM Ref 78/38/375
Artist Fred Taylor
Displayed 1910

Plate 23

Company	North London Railway
Title	Open Air Route
Displayed	1910
Printer	McCorquodale & Co Limited, Cardington St, London, NW
Size	63cm × 100cm
NRM Ref	78/38/1080

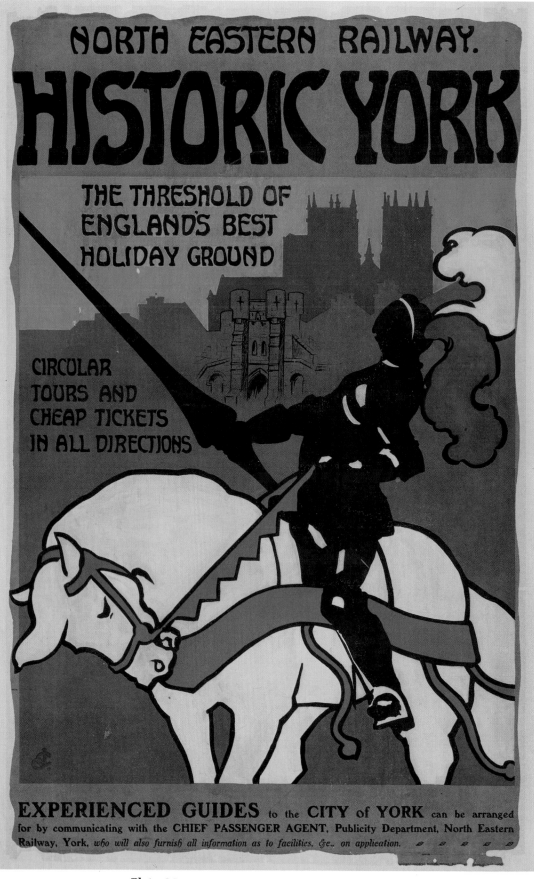

Plate 24

Company   North Eastern Railway
Title   Historic York
Displayed Circa 1910
Printer   'Guardian' General Printing Works, Manchester, Reddish and London
Size   63cm × 102cm
NRM Ref   79/38/306

Plate 25

Company	Caledonian Railway and London & North Western Railway
Title	Come to Scotland for your Holidays by the West Coast Route
Displayed	Circa 1909
Size	63cm × 99cm
NRM Ref	86/38/44

51

Plate 26

Company	Great Central Railway	Printer	Chorley & Pickersgill Ltd, The Electric Press, Leeds & London
Title	Step on at Grimsby for the Continent	Size	125cm × 100cm
Artist	Attributed to Frank Mason	NRM Ref	86/38/316
Displayed	1911		

Plate 27

Company	North Eastern Railway
Title	Hornsea. Lake-Land by the Sea
Artist	C W Loten
Displayed	1911
Printer	Brumby & Clarke Ltd, Hull & London
Size	64cm × 102cm
NRM Ref	86/38/187

Plate 28

Company	Great Eastern Railway	Printer	David Allen & Sons Ltd, Harrow
Title	Parkeston Quay, Harwich	Size	126cm × 101cm
Artist	Norman Wilkinson	NRM Ref	78/38/474
Displayed	Circa 1912		

Plate 29

Company   Caledonian Railway
Title   Bridge of Allan
Displayed Circa 1912
Printer   Dobson Molle & Co Ltd, Edinburgh & London
Size   75cm × 103cm
NRM Ref   87/38/290

Plate 30

Company   Great Central Railway
Title   England's Latest Port. Immingham (Grimsby) Deep Water Dock
Artist   Attributed to Fortunino Matania
Displayed 1912

Printer   The Avenue Press Ltd,
          6 Bouverie St, London, EC
Size   126cm × 102cm
NRM Ref   86/38/97

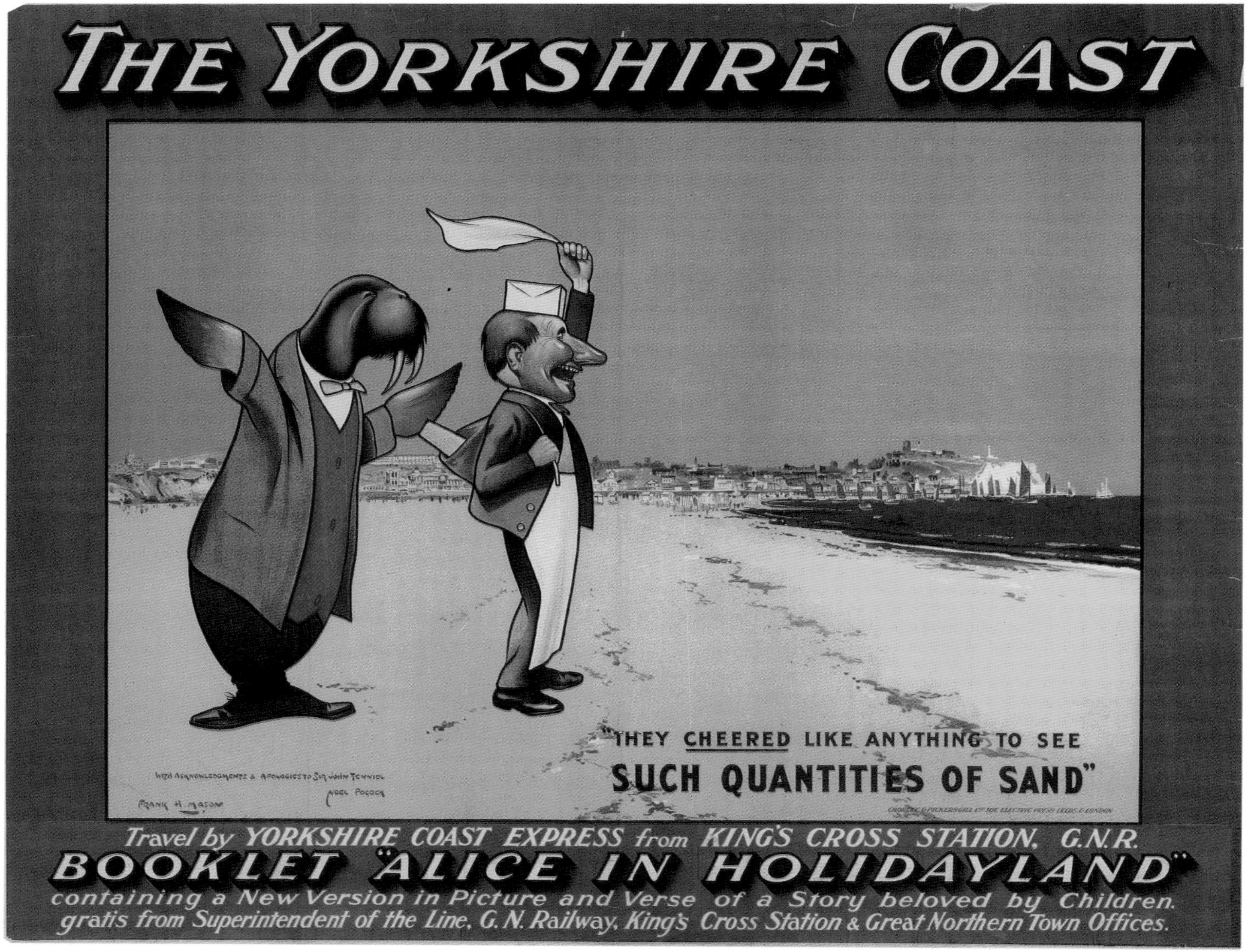
THE YORKSHIRE COAST
"THEY CHEERED LIKE ANYTHING TO SEE
SUCH QUANTITIES OF SAND"
With Acknowledgements & Apologies to Sir John Tenniel
Noel Pocock
Frank H. Mason
Travel by YORKSHIRE COAST EXPRESS from KING'S CROSS STATION, G.N.R.
BOOKLET "ALICE IN HOLIDAYLAND"
containing a New Version in Picture and Verse of a Story beloved by Children.
gratis from Superintendent of the Line, G.N. Railway, King's Cross Station & Great Northern Town Offices.

Plate 31

Company	Great Northern Railway	*Printer*	Chorley & Pickersgill Ltd, The Electric Press, Leeds & London
Title	The Yorkshire Coast. The Walrus and the Carpenter	*Size*	126cm × 100cm
Artist	Frank H Mason	*NRM Ref*	86/38/236
Displayed	1913		

THE YORKSHIRE COAST

Write Passenger Manager, Advertising Section, North Eastern Railway, York for a free copy of

BOOKLET "ALICE IN HOLIDAYLAND"

containing a New Version in Picture and Verse of a Story beloved by Children.

Plate 32

Company	North Eastern Railway	Printer	The Arden Press, Letchworth
Title	The Yorkshire Coast. Tweedledum and Tweedledee	Size	125cm × 100cm
Artist	Frank H Mason	NRM Ref	86/38/247
Displayed	1913		

Plate 33

Company	South Eastern & Chatham Railway
Title	The Breezy Kent Coast. 'Caesar's Choice'
Artist	Graham Phillips
Displayed	1913
Printer	McCorquodale & Co Ltd, London
Size	63cm × 100cm
NRM Ref	75/38/42

Plate 34

Company	North Eastern Railway
Title	Bright Breezy Bracing Bridlington
Displayed	Circa 1913
Printer	Petty & Sons Ltd, Whitehall Printeries, Leeds
Size	64cm × 102cm
NRM Ref	86/38/182

Plate 35

Company   South Eastern & Chatham Railway
Title   American Line. Southampton to New York via Cherbourg
Displayed   1913
Printer   Sir Joseph Causton & Sons Limited, London
Size   62cm × 101cm
NRM Ref   79/38/360

Plate 36

Company	North Eastern Railway
Title	Bright Breezy Bracing Bridlington
Displayed	Circa 1913
Printer	Petty & Sons Ltd, Leeds, London & Reading

Size 127cm × 102cm

NRM Ref 86/38/244

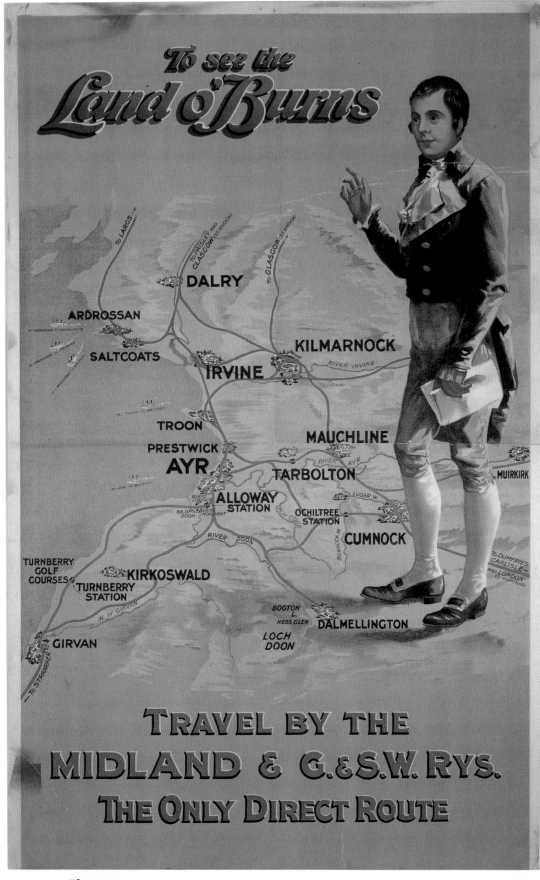

Plate 37

Company   Midland Railway and Glasgow & South Western Railway
Title   To see the Land o'Burns
Displayed 1914
Printer   Andrew Reid & Company Ltd, 50 Grey Street, Newcastle-on-Tyne
Size   64cm × 102cm
NRM Ref   78/38/1077

Plate 38

Company   Midland & Great Northern Joint Railway
Title   Restful Holidays on Quiet Waters. Norfolk Rivers and Broads
Displayed   1914
Printer   Photochrom Co Ltd, London

Size   121cm × 95cm
NRM Ref   76/38/64

Plate 39

Company	Isle of Wight Railway and Isle of Wight Central Railway
Title	England's Garden Isle
Displayed	1914
Size	64cm × 102cm
NRM Ref	83/38/3

Plate 40

Company North Eastern Railway
Title The Magic of the Yorkshire Dales
Displayed 1914
Printer Andrew Reid & Co Ltd, 50 Grey St, Newcastle-on-Tyne

Size 127cm × 102cm
NRM Ref 86/38/243

NORTH STAFFORDSHIRE RAILWAY

RUDYARD LAKE

200 ACRES OF WATER

Boating & Fishing

Golfing amidst Charming Scenery

Much care has been bestowed by the COMPANY upon the extension and development of RUDYARD, which is now certainly one of the most attractive **HOLIDAY RESORTS** in the country. A BEAUTIFUL WALK has been laid out from RUDYARD LAKE STATION leading along the margin of the water through Cliffe Park.

BOATS may be hired on reasonable terms. FISHING TICKETS may be obtained from the Station Master. Excellent Hotel and Catering Arrangements.

The **GOLF COURSE** is situated at the North end of the LAKE, close to RUDYARD LAKE Station.

SHERWIN & Co. (Hanley), Limited.

Plate 41

Company	North Staffordshire Railway
Title	Rudyard Lake
Displayed	1915
Printer	Sherwin & Co (Hanley), Limited
Size	63cm × 101cm
NRM Ref	86/38/88

67

Plate 42

Company	Great Northern Railway
Title	Harrogate. Britain's Health Resort
Displayed	Circa 1921
Printer	Thos Forman & Sons, Nottingham
Size	64cm × 102cm
NRM Ref	86/38/90

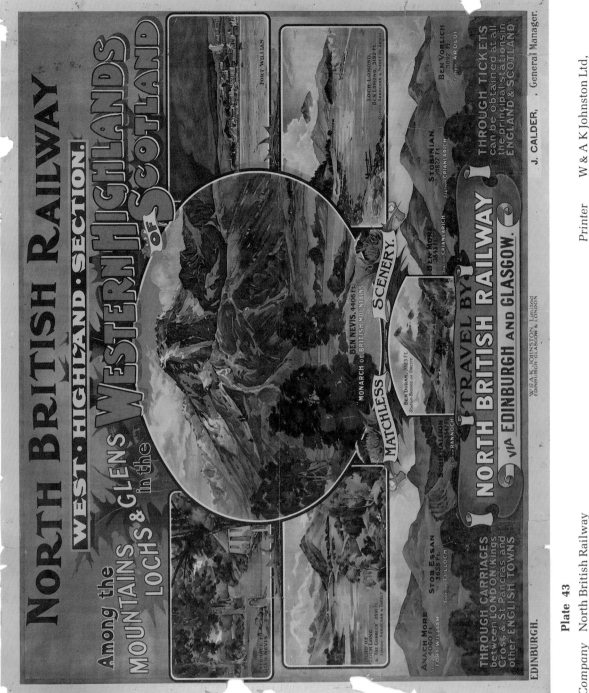

Plate 43

Company   North British Railway
Title   Among the Mountains, Lochs and Glens in the Western Highlands of
          Scotland
Displayed Circa 1921

Printer   W & A K Johnston Ltd,
           Edinburgh, Glasgow & London
Size   127cm × 102cm
NRM Ref   86/38/95

Plate 44

Company	South Eastern & Chatham Railway
Title	Crystal Palace Grand International Show of Poultry & Pigeons
Displayed	1921
Printer	Haycock, Cadle & Graham Ltd, Camberwell, SE5
Size	64cm × 102cm
NRM Ref	79/38/358

Plate 45

Company	Lancashire & Yorkshire Railway
Title	Southport for Mild Winters
Displayed	Circa 1921
Printer	Horrocks & Co Ltd, Ashton under Lyne

Size	127cm × 102cm
NRM Ref	79/38/306

EXPRESS RESTAURANT CAR TRAINS between KING'S CROSS & HARROGATE

HARROGATE

BRITAIN'S 100% SPA

ILLUSTRATED BROCHURE free on application to any G.N.R. Office or Superintendent of the Line, King's Cross Station, London, N.1.

Plate 46

Company	Great Northern Railway
Title	Harrogate. Britain's 100% Spa
Displayed	Circa 1921
Printer	Hill, Siffken & Co, London
Size	61cm × 100cm
NRM Ref	86/38/89

72

Plate 47

Company   Great Central Railway   Printer   McCaw, Stevenson & Orr Ltd, London & Belfast
Title   Blackpool for Gorgeous Sights   Size   126cm × 100cm
Artist   Wilton Williams   NRM Ref 86/38/18
Displayed Circa 1922

MILLER'S DALE

The Peak District for Picture Makers

Particulars on application to the
Midland Railway Coy., Derby.

Plate 48

Company	Midland Railway
Title	The Peak District for Picture Makers
Artist	C E Turner
Displayed	Circa 1922
Printer	Hudson & Kearns Ltd, London
Size	63cm × 101cm
NRM Ref	76/38/5